FISH FACES

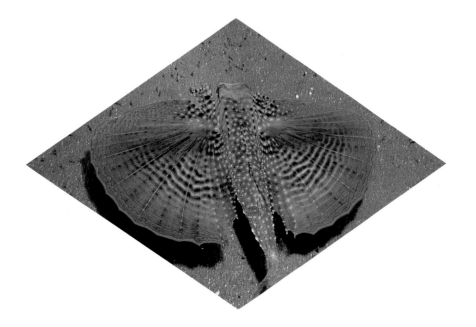

To Howard Hall, Mark Conlin, Bob Cranston,
and Marty Snyderman, for the good times

Acknowledgments

My sincere thanks go to Dr. Richard Rosenblatt, H. J. Walker, Cindy Klepallo, and Ken Smith at Scripps Institution of Oceanography for teaching me all I know about ichthyology. The following individuals and organizations provided me with access to the world's best diving: Dive Taveuni and the *Pacific Nomad* in Fiji, the Seychelles Ministry of Tourism, David and Glynnis Rowat at the Seychelles Underwater Center, Samson Shak and Ron Holland of Borneo Divers, Luchi de la Cruz, Tim Sevilla, and Karina Escudero of Divemate Philippines, and Gwen Roland at *Scuba Times* magazine. Dan Walsh, Dan Auber, Brandon Cole, Burt Jones, Randall Kosaki, Jackie Young, and James Watt have been great buddies, both underwater and above. Further thanks go to Adrienne Betz and Simone Kaplan, my editors, who supported my ideas and helped organize them into this book.

Henry Holt and Company, LLC, *Publishers since 1866*
175 Fifth Avenue, New York, New York 10010
www.henryholtchildrensbooks.com

Henry Holt® is a registered trademark of Henry Holt and Company, LLC.
Copyright © 1993 by Norbert Wu. All rights reserved.
Distributed in Canada by H. B. Fenn and Company Ltd.

Library of Congress Cataloging-in-Publication Data
Wu, Norbert. Fish faces / Norbert Wu.
Summary: The author-photographer, a marine biologist, uses his own photographs to introduce readers to some of the more amusing characteristics of the creatures he's encountered on his dives.
1. Fishes—Juvenile literature. [1. Fishes. 2. Marine biology.]
I. Title   QL617.2.W82   1993   597—dc20   92-27343

ISBN-13: 978-0-8050-5347-0 / ISBN-10: 0-8050-5347-6
13 15 17 19 20 18 16 14 12

Published in hardcover in 1993 by Henry Holt and Company
First paperback edition—1997

Manufactured in China

FISH FACES

N O R B E R T   W U

Henry Holt and Company ◆ **New York**

4

One fish, two fish, three fish, more
Fish that dart and dip and slide

Fish that glide on fins like wings

Flat fish, round fish
A very long and thin fish

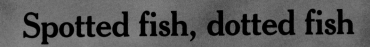

Fish with lines and stripes and waves

Fish with spikes and spines and branches

Fish with mouths that open wide
Mouth like a tube, mouth like a beak
Mouth that belongs to a monster of the deep

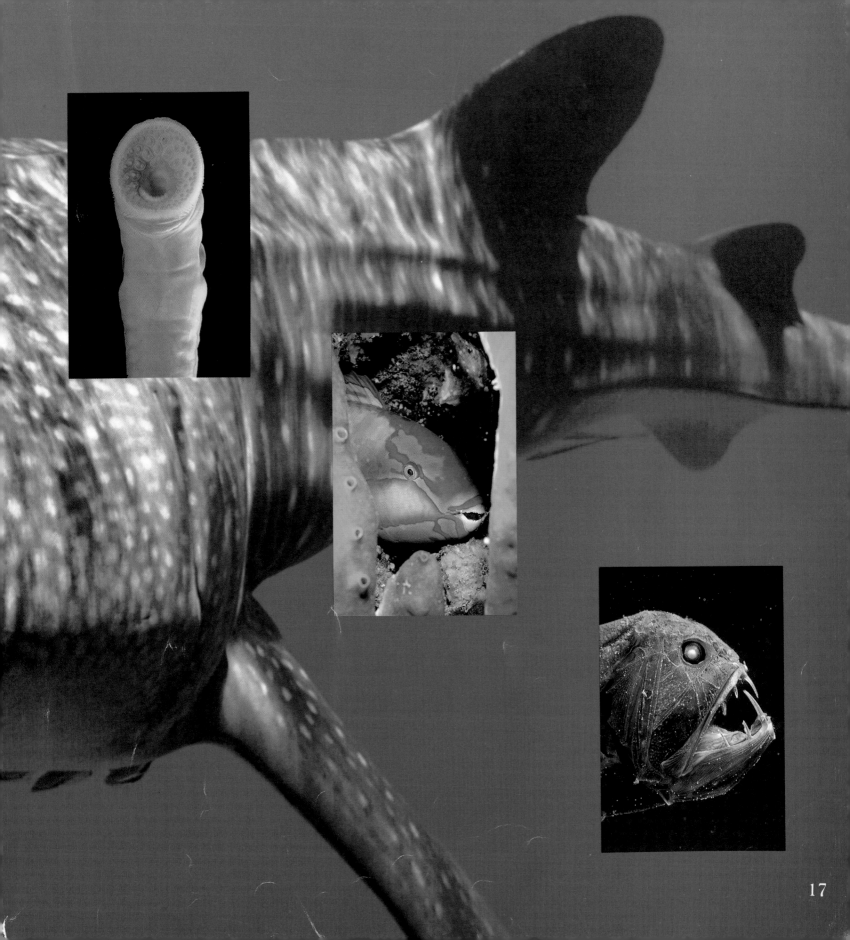

A long nose, a flat nose, a hard-to-ignore nose
A nose that looks like it could cut wood
A nose that shines in the dark!

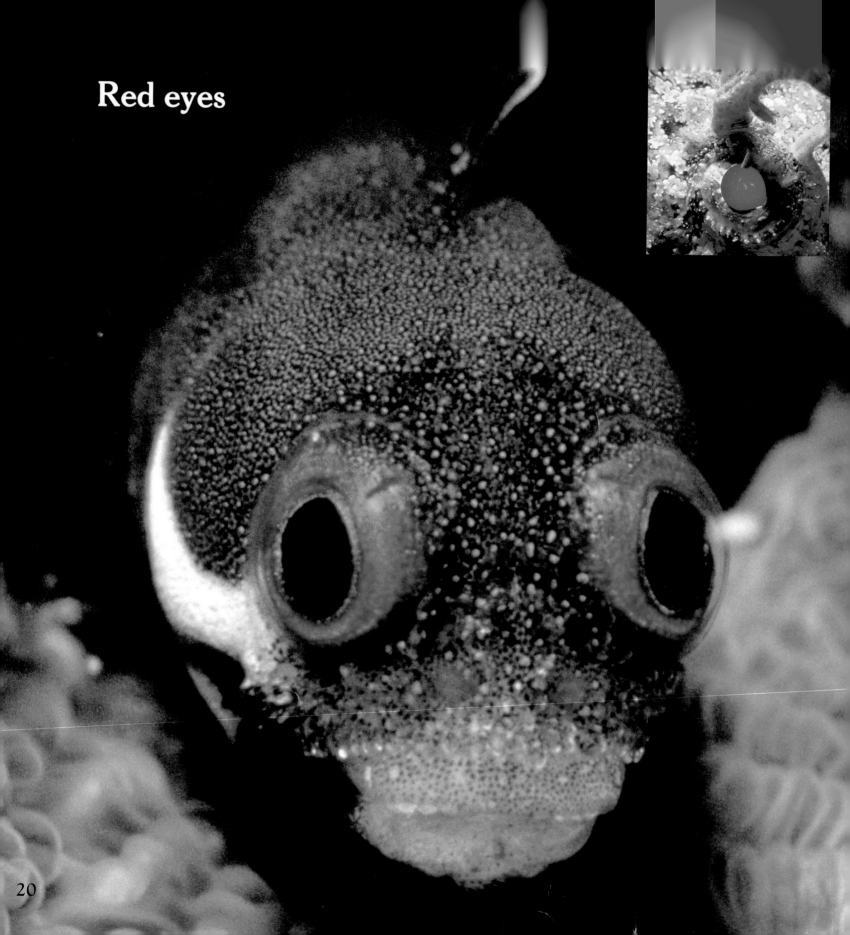

Red eyes

Green eyes

21

Great big pretend eyes

Eyes that are hooded

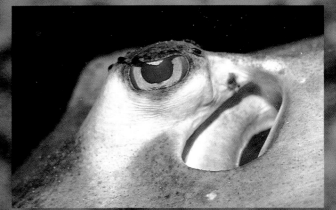

Eyes that shine

Eyes that stick up like periscopes

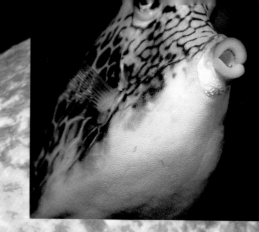

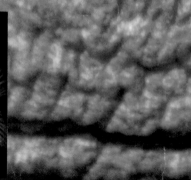

Faces that are fier⬤

Faces that could be sad or mad